MW00443786

Breakfast in Bed

Treat Your Woman Like the Queen She Is

by

A Kitchen Slave
(Paulo L'Amour)

Welcome

I am a kitchen slave. I live to serve my Queen. Most mornings my precious Mistress desires breakfast in bed before she begins her arduous day, and I gladly satisfy her. She works her fingers to the bone and deserves to be pampered. She is the life force of our home.

Only the best will do for her.

I have dedicated my time to the study of food and that which satisfies my True Love. These are her favorite breakfast and brunch meals. These recipes have garnered me much favor. Selfish of me, you say? Looking for favors from my Queen? I admit my weakness. I long for her...approval.

Sometimes my Mistress rewards me for my efforts. Those are my days of pure bliss. If you prepare these recipes for your own True Love, perhaps you will be rewarded as well.

Repeat this mantra often if you desire to please your woman and reap the rewards she has to offer you...

"I live to serve my Queen. I am her breakfast Slave. I willingly go to the kitchen to prepare the treats she so greatly deserves to enjoy in bed."

Contents

This cookbook has been
approved by my Queen in
its entirety.

I hope she will reward me.

Crepes for my Queen

Crepes are a traditional French cuisine, but I do not care. I only care that my adorable Queen loves them. A crepe is essentially a very thin pancake that can be served alone or stuffed with all manner of delicious morsels. Wheat flour is conventional for savory crepes, but non-wheat flours will do just as well for my Mistress. I only care for the results and her rewards. These are some of her favorites and those for which I have been the most rewarded.

Scallops and Cream Stuffed Crepes

Ingredients for the Crepes

- 2/3 cup wheat flour
- 1 cup milk
- 1 tablespoon olive oil
- 1 teaspoon sugar
- ¼ teaspoon baking powder
- 1 pinch salt
- 1 egg
- 1 teaspoon butter

Ingredients for the Filling

- 2 tablespoons butter
- ½ pound scallops, chopped
- 3 ounces almonds, chopped
- 1 cup spinach, chopped
- 1 small poblano pepper, chopped
- ½ small onion
- ¼ cup cream
- 6 ounces cream cheese
- 1 cup shredded cheese (Monterrey Jack is wonderful, but Cheddar is good, too, depending on your True Love's preference)

Cooking Directions for the Crepes

1. Add all crepe ingredients except butter to a large mixing bowl. Mix well until the batter is smooth.
2. Heat crepe pan or small skillet to medium heat. Add butter and melt.
3. Add about 3 tablespoons of batter to the crepe pan and spread until batter covers entire surface.
4. Cook about 2 minutes or until the bottom is lightly browned.
5. Flip and cook about 30 seconds to 1 minute or until light brown.
6. Continue until all the crepes are completed.
7. Set crepes aside and cover until ready for use.

Cooking Directions for the Filling

1. Heat a sauté pan to medium heat. Add butter, poblano pepper and onion.
2. Cook about 5 minutes or until vegetables soften.
3. Add the nuts, spinach and chopped scallops. Stir.
4. Cook 3 minutes or until scallops are cooked through and spinach is wilted.
5. Add the cream cheese and heavy cream.
6. Cook, stirring often, until cheese is melted. Remove from heat.
7. Preheat oven to 350 degrees.
8. Scoop about ¼ cup of your filling mixture into each crepe. Roll the crepe.
9. Set the crepes into 11x7 inch baking dish that has been lightly buttered.
10. Top with shredded cheese.
11. Bake about 10 minutes or until cheese is melted.
12. Serve to your wondrous Queen with love.

- -

I prepare this for my Queen because she craves the ocean, and I crave to swim in the warm pools of her eyes. Perhaps she will allow me to dive beneath the covers with her when she is done.

- -

11. For the Maple-Kiwi-Chili Sauce: In a sauce pan, add butter and melt.
12. Stir in corn starch to form a roux.
13. Add orange juice and maple syrup. Stir.
14. Bring to a boil and reduce heat to a light boil - keep about 2 minutes to thicken.
15. Remove from heat and allow to cool slightly, about 3 minutes.
16. Stir in kiwi slices and chili peppers and serve!

Oh, the tang and the tart citrus of the Kiwi, so much like my True Love as she curls her toes beneath the covers, taunting me with her delicious gaze. Pray your mistress finishes this quickly, and then moves onto you.

Fruit, So Succulent – Just Like My Sweet

The sweetness of my Queen is beyond comparison, but if pressed, I would compare her to the wondrous sweet-tart of the adorable apple, the powerful burst of the succulent strawberry, the regality of the finest cherry, and the lusciousness of the perfect pineapple. If you serve your Queen these breakfast fruits, perhaps she will allow you to sample her ripe pleasures.

Tropical Fruit with Vanilla-Pineapple Syrup

Ingredients

- 1/3 cup sugar
- 1/4 cup pineapple juice
- 1 teaspoon vanilla extract
- 1 cup chopped pineapple
- 1 kiwi, peeled and sliced
- 1 small mango, peeled and chopped
- 2 teaspoons fresh lime juice

Cooking Directions

1. In a saucepan, add sugar, pineapple juice and ¼ cup water. Stir it all up to combine.
2. Bring to a feisty boil, then reduce heat to low and simmer for 10 minutes, stirring occasionally, until mixture reduces by about a third.
3. Remove from heat and cool. It will get nice and thick for you. Add to a container and chill in the refrigerator until ready to use.
4. On a beautiful serving place, arrange all of your sweet fruit so that your Queen finds it palatable. Drizzle with the syrup you've made and serve it to her in bed.

Sweetened bananas drive my Queen wild, and that is exactly how I want her. There is nothing more satisfying than a wild Queen in the bedroom. Will your True Love get a little wild for you with this recipe?

Eggs to Perfection

The egg is the ideal breakfast food. Perfect, just like my One True Love. The egg symbolizes everything pure that is life, that is hope, that is alive. This is how I feel when I watch my Mistress devour an egg, so filled with vitality and desire. Will these egg offerings bring me into her bed? I can only pray.

Avocado Soufflés

Ingredients

- 1 small ripe avocado
- 1 tablespoons butter
- 1 tablespoons flour
- 6 tablespoons heavy cream + 1 table-spoon
- 2 eggs, separated
- 1 teaspoon Key lime juice
- Salt to taste

Cooking Directions

1. Peel the skin from the tender avocado and chop. Transfer to a blender.
2. Add 1 tablespoon heavy cream and Key lime juice. Blend to form a puree. Transfer to a mixing bowl.
3. Preheat oven to 375 degrees. Heat a large pan to medium heat and add butter and flour. Mix to form a roux.
4. Add remaining cream and stir until consistent. Remove from heat and transfer to mixing bowl. To mixing bowl, add egg yolks and salt to taste. Mix well.
5. In a separate bowl, add egg whites and beat with a hand mixer on high about 5 minutes, or until the whites are fluffy and form stiff peaks. Ahh, stiff peaks. They are so much better when they are stiff. I digress…
6. In small batches, fold the egg whites into the egg-roux-avocado mixture. Do this very gently, as not to compromise the fluffiness of the egg whites. Pretend you are caressing your one True Love.
7. Once completed, gently transfer mixture into lightly oiled small ramekins or into a larger baking dish.
8. Bake for 20-25 minutes, or until cooked through and still slightly moist in the middle. You can check with a toothpick.
9. Serve to your Love in bed.

This omelet explodes with flavor. Don't you want to explode? My Mistress adores being served omelets that are rolled up and sliced. It's fun to do something a little different. Will your Queen do something different for you?

Eggs in the Hole

Ingredients

- 2 large eggs
- 2 slices bread
- 2 teaspoons soft goat cheese

- Salt and pepper to taste
- 1 tablespoon butter

Cooking Directions

1. Slice circles out of the middles of the bread. It's easiest to do this with a coffee cup rim, or the rim of a small glass. Special bonus points for you if you use a heart shaped cookie cutter. You want special bonus points, don't you?
2. Heat a frying pan to medium heat and add 1 tablespoon butter. Allow to melt, like your Mistress melts your heart.
3. Set bread onto pan and lightly toast about 1 minute each side.
4. Crack an egg into the holed-out center of each toast slice and season with salt and pepper.
5. Fry about 2 minutes, then flip and cook another minute, or to your liking.
6. Transfer to a plate and top with circular (or heart shaped) toast middle sections.
7. Top with sprinklings of goat cheese and serve to your Queen in bed.

This is the cutest little recipe with a variety of names, so cute like my Queen. I could make so many comments here about the name, but my Mistress prefers me not to be vulgar. I am not vulgar. I am simply in love and filled with desire for my True Love. I must express myself with food.

Poached Eggs Over Caprese Salad

Ingredients

- 1 English muffin or thin roll, lightly toasted
- 1 small Roma tomato
- 1 ounce mozzarella cheese
- 6 basil leaves, chopped + extra whole leaves for garnish
- 6 slices pepperoni
- ¼ cup balsamic vinegar
- 1 teaspoon sugar
- 2 eggs
- 1 tablespoon white vinegar

Cooking Directions

1. Set the toasted muffin halves onto a serving plate for your Queen.
2. Slice the Roma tomato into 6 thick slices and set them onto the toasted muffins.
3. Slice the mozzarella cheese into thin ½ ounce slices. Set them on top of the tomatoes.
4. Top with pepperoni slices and pieces of chopped basil.
5. Add balsamic vinegar and sugar to a pot and bring to a slight boil. Reduce heat and simmer until reduced. Remove from heat and cool. It will thicken.
6. Meanwhile, add some water to a large pot with the vinegar. Bring to a slight boil.
7. Crack eggs into the water and poach about 4 minutes, or until egg whites are cooked through. Set eggs on top of pepperoni and basil slices.
8. Drizzle Balsamic vinegar reduction over the bites on the plate.
9. Serve to your Queen in bed.

Extra points for you if you use fresh ingredients from the garden, like I do. My Queen loves fresh ingredients. I hope she will also love me after sampling this meal in the bedroom. This is a breakfast version of a traditional Caprese salad that your True Love will adore. Will she adore you? Reward you?

Pepper-Asparagus Frittata

Ingredients

- 6 eggs
- 1-1/2 cups asparagus, chopped
- 1 red bell pepper, chopped
- 4 small potatoes, baked
- 1 teaspoon fresh garlic, minced
- 1 cup white cheddar cheese, shredded
- 2 tablespoons smoked paprika
- 1 tablespoon dried basil
- Salt and pepper to taste
- Spray oil
- Hot sauce of choice for serving

Cooking Directions

1. Preheat oven to 350 degrees.
2. In a 6x9 pan, lightly coat with spray oil and mash the baked potatoes until they fill the bottom evenly. You can keep the skins or discard them if you prefer.
3. Sprinkle with paprika, dried basil and salt and pepper to taste.
4. Heat a large pan to medium heat and coat with spray oil. Add asparagus and red bell pepper and cook about 5 minutes, or until vegetables begin to soften.
5. Add garlic and stir. Cook 1 more minute. Remove from heat and allow to cool.
6. Spread shredded cheese over the potato mixture.
7. Spread vegetable mixture over cheddar cheese.
8. In a mixing bowl, add eggs and beat well.
9. Pour over the top of the vegetable mixture and allow to evenly spread through.
10. Bake 20-25 minutes.
11. Allow to cool, then top with hot sauce and serve to your Queen in bed.

The colors in this frittata are wondrous to behold, just like my wondrous Queen. The strong, firm eggs that result here are like my Mistress' thighs, so delectable, so inviting.

Mini Muffin Frittatas

Ingredients

- 12 eggs, beaten
- 10 ounces Mexican style cheese
- 6 ounces cooked chorizo
- 2 jalapeno peppers, diced
- Sliced avocado to serve
- Spray oil

Cooking Directions

1. Preheat oven to 350 degrees.
2. Lightly oil 12 muffin or cupcakes pans.
3. In a mixing bowl, combine eggs, cheese, chorizo and jalapeno peppers.
4. Pour into muffin tins and bake 15 minutes.
5. Serve over sliced avocado to your Queen in bed.

My adorable Queen, may these mini frittatas cooked in the daintiest of muffin tins make your muffin more accessible to me. I can no longer disguise my desire for you.

White Cheese and Pepperoni Omelets

Ingredients

- 2 eggs, beaten
- 1/4 cup Mozzarella cheese
- 1/4 cup Feta cheese, crumbled
- 6 pepperoni slices, quartered

- 1 teaspoon chili powder
- Salt and pepper to taste
- Spray oil
- Hot sauce to taste

Cooking Directions

1. Heat a frying pan to medium-high heat and coat lightly with spray oil.
2. Spread pepperoni slices over pan and cook about 30 seconds.
3. Add beaten eggs and tilt pan to even out the egg mixture. Cook 30 seconds, or until eggs begin to set.
4. Add cheeses, chili powder and salt and pepper.
5. Fold sides of eggs over the cheeses and flip.
6. Cook about 1 minute, or until eggs are cooked through and cheeses are nicely melted.
7. Serve with your favorite hot sauce and serve to your Queen in bed.

To my Mistress: When the cheeses melt and coalesce around the slices of pepperoni in this flavorful omelet, will you reward me with your embrace? Perhaps a kiss? Perhaps more? Now it is my heart that is melting.

The Ultimate Cheesy Jalapeno-Ham Omelet

Ingredients

- 1 egg
- 1 jalapeno pepper, diced
- 1 ounce cooked ham, diced
- 1.5 ounces shredded cheddar cheese
- 1.5 ounces shredded Chihuahua cheese
- 1/4 avocado, sliced for topping
- Salt and pepper to taste

Cooking Directions

1. Preheat an 8-inch pan to medium heat and lightly coat with oil.
2. Add ham and jalapeno pepper. Cook about 5 minutes to soften. Set aside.
3. Beat egg in a bowl and add to hot pan. Rotate the pan a bit to allow the egg to spread evenly over the pan.
4. Sprinkle with salt and pepper to taste and cook about 1 minute, or until egg is set and no longer liquid.
5. Add jalapeno and ham mixture to the center of the egg.
6. Add cheese and fold egg in half over the top of the jalapeno-ham-cheese mixture and press lightly. Basically, you are enclosing the contents within the egg.
7. Cook about 30 seconds longer, or until cheese melts.
8. Transfer to a plate, top with avocado slices and serve to your Queen in the bedroom.

Oh Queen, my beautiful Queen. I adore that you love this basic cheese-filled omelet with ham and simple avocado slices. So easy to prepare, so easy to serve you in bed. May I join you under the covers once you are done with your meal? I also need nourishment…

Pancakes and Toasts

Sometimes my Mistress wants something more traditional, like French Toast or simple pancakes. She says these bring her back to her wild days when life was carefree and so was she. I will serve her like she needs to be served, and perhaps some of that wild streak will come back to my Queen and I will reap the benefits.

Thick French Toast with Spicy Rum Butter

Ingredients

- 4 one-inch thick slices of multigrain bread
- 3 eggs
- 1/3 cup milk
- ½ teaspoon vanilla
- Pinch of sugar

- *For the Spicy Rum Butter*
- ½ stick butter (2 ounces)
- ¼ cup brown sugar
- 2 teaspoons spiced rum
- 1 teaspoon chili powder

Cooking Directions

1. In a mixing bowl, beat the eggs with milk, vanilla and sugar.
2. Soak the bread in the egg mixture.
3. Heat a frying pan to medium heat and cook each piece of bread about 1-2 minutes per side, or until they are nice and brown. Do not burn.
4. Prepare butter by softening the butter. Cream with brown sugar, spiced rum and chili powder.
5. Serve over the top of your hot French toast and carry to your Queen in bed.

My True Love is so sassy and spicy. This offering matches her level of fieriness with a tingling rum butter that will win her heart. Is your Mistress spicy as well? If not, you can skip the chili powder, but My Mistress enjoys the tingle on her tongue. Oh, the images those words bring to my mind…

My Queen is quite fond of this simple breakfast. She calls each bite her delicious little morsels. Little does she know that I call her the very same thing. In my mind. I must never speak this aloud to my Mistress. But she is my delicious little morsel. I must treat her so.

My Queen's Meaty Omelet with Pico de Gallo

Ingredients

- 2 slices bacon
- 2 breakfast sausage links, chopped
- 2 ounces breakfast ham, diced
- 2 large eggs
- Salt and pepper to taste
- FOR THE PICO DE GALLO

- 1/2 small onion, chopped
- 1 small tomato, chopped
- 1 tablespoon fresh chopped cilantro
- 1 small jalapeno pepper, diced
- 1 clove garlic, minced
- Salt and pepper to taste

Cooking Directions

1. Prepare the pico de gallo by combining onion, tomato, cilantro, jalapeno, garlic and a bit of salt and pepper in a small mixing bowl. Mix well. Cover and refrigerate until ready to use.
2. Heat a large pan to medium heat and add bacon. Cook about 5 minutes.
3. Add the chopped sausage to the pan and continue to cook. Go about 5 minutes or so, checking on the bacon so it doesn't burn. Break apart the bacon with a wooden spoon so it mixes all up nicely with the delicious sausage.
4. Add the ham and cook about a minute longer.
5. Set your meat aside until ready to use.
6. Scramble up your eggs in a separate small mixing bowl.
7. Return the same pan to medium heat. It should still be nice and oily from the bacon. Add the scrambled eggs and turn the pan so the eggs coat the entire bottom.
8. Add salt and pepper to taste. My Queen prefers only a dash of each, but be careful. The bacon already has a bit of salt.
9. Cook about 1-2 minutes, or until the egg begins to set.
10. Add your meat mixture to the middle of the eggs, but just off to the side a bit. Fold the

egg over with a spatula to cover the meat mixture. It should be a nice and neat fold for your Mistress. It must look pretty. Do not fail her.

11. Cook about 30 seconds longer, or until the eggs are set.
12. Carefully set your meaty omelet onto a pretty serving dish then top with a bit of the pico de gallo.
13. Serve to your Queen in bed with an extra helping of love.

Now your Queen can have an extra helping of meat for her breakfast or brunch while waiting for you in the bedroom. No doubt she will curl her toes as the odors of the bacon, sausage and ham waft through the air to her. The pico de gallo will burst in her mouth with just the right amount of heat and spice. Make it your life to be there to embrace the aftermath of gratitude.

Petite Filet Mignon and Egg with Simple Hollandaise Sauce

Ingredients

- 1 4-ounce filet mignon
- A bit of olive oil
- Salt and pepper to taste
- 1 large egg
- 1 tablespoon butter
- FOR THE HOLLANDAISE

- 3 egg yolks
- Pinch of cayenne powder
- 2 tablespoons fresh lemon juice
- ½ cup butter, melted
- Salt and pepper to taste

Cooking Directions

1. Heat a grill pan to medium-high heat. Lightly brush with olive oil.
2. Season your Queen's filet mignon with salt and pepper.
3. Add the filet to the pan and grill for 3 minutes, until a nice crust forms on the bottom.
4. Flip and cook another 3 minutes, or until cooked to your Mistress's preference. My Mistress loves her steaks very rare.
5. Set steak aside to rest.
6. While steak is resting, heat a small pan to medium heat and add 1 tablespoon butter. Allow to melt.
7. Add egg and season with salt and pepper. Cook about 3 minutes, or until egg begins to set, then flip and cook an additional minute to cook through while keeping the yolk nice and liquid.
8. Top the steak with the egg.

9. Now, prepare your Hollandaise sauce thusly – To a blender, add egg yolks, salt and pepper, and lemon juice. Blend for about 3 seconds on high.
10. Pour in melted butter a bit at a time and pulse continuously to combine. Once the butter is all combined, it should be nice and creamy.
11. Remove to a bowl but leave behind the milky remains. Season with cayenne and adjust with salt, pepper and more lemon juice if your Queen desires.
12. Drizzle the Hollandaise over your egg and filet and serve to your Queen in bed with love and devotion.

Your Queen will adore you for this quick and easy Hollandaise sauce over the perfect filet mignon. She will think of you as her little French chef and perhaps that will inspire her to whisper French words in your ear. Who cares what those words are. They will sound sexy no matter what.

Sausage and Egg Croissant with Gouda

Ingredients

- 1 croissant, sliced in half
- 1 thick breakfast sausage patty
- 1 large egg
- 1 slice Gouda cheese – be sure to slice it thinly to fit the croissant
- Salt and pepper to taste

Cooking Directions

1. Heat a pan to medium heat and add the sausage patty. Cook about 3 minutes and then flip. Continue to cook until patty is cooked thoroughly through, about 3-4 more minutes. Your time will vary by the thickness. Do not fail your Queen. Remove from heat and set atop the bottom slice of the croissant.
2. Crack the egg into the same pan, still heated to medium. The pan should be coated with the oils from the sausage. If not, add a bit of butter or oil first.
3. Scramble the egg in the pan and swirl to coat. Sprinkle in a bit of salt and pepper. Cook about a minute or so until the eggs begins to set.
4. Fold the egg in half, and then in half again so that it will fit the size of the croissant you've chosen for your True Love.
5. Remove the egg from the pan with a spatula and set it atop the sausage patty.
6. Top with Gouda cheese and add everything to a toaster oven. Toast lightly about 3 minutes to melt the cheese and lightly toast the croissant.
7. Set onto a beautiful serving plate and carry to your Queen in the bedroom. Serve her willingly.

My Queen loves this simple yet meaty breakfast croissant because it reminds her of a tiny little place we frequent in the winters. And, my Mistress loves her morning meat. Oh, my entire body just quivered. My Mistress, may I serve you again? And again? And again?

The Country Girl

Ah, the Southwest, that wondrous land of the exciting and profound, of culinary delight. It is so much like my Mistress, my gorgeous Queen. With this recipe I bring her the flavors of the Southwest, and perhaps she will reward me with her love.

Breakfast Grits

Ingredients

- 2 slices bacon
- ½ small white onion, chopped
- 1 tablespoon butter
- ½ cup stone ground grits
- 1 cup water (or more as needed)
- Pinch of salt
- ¼ cup shredded cheddar cheese + more for topping
- 1 large egg
- 1 teaspoon vinegar
- Ground pepper

Cooking Directions

1. Heat a pan to medium heat and add bacon. Cook about 5 minutes, then flip and cook a few minutes more, until bacon is nice and crispy. Remove from pan and drain on paper towels.
2. Heat a large pot to medium heat and add onion and butter. Cook about 5 minutes, or until onion is softened.
3. Add grits, water and salt. Bring to a boil then reduce heat to simmer. Cover and cook about 40 minutes, or until grits are cooked through. If your grits become too thick, add a bit more water and stir.
4. Remove from heat and cool slightly.
5. Crumble the cooked bacon and add to grits. Add ¼ cup cheddar cheese and stir.
6. Next, poach an egg by bringing a few cups of water to a boil. Add the vinegar and crack the egg into the water. Lightly poach the egg about 4 minutes, or until the egg is cooked through and set, but the yolk still nice and soft.
7. Spoon the grits onto a pretty serving plate then top with the poached egg.
8. Sprinkle with black pepper and serve to your Queen in bed with your undying devotion.

Grits get my Queen giddy, so I will bring her grits as often as she likes. When she is giddy, she is adorable and sweet and free with her adorations. I pray she will adore me as I adore her. Will your Queen adore you for this meal?

Liquored and Lubed

Drinks! Better chance of getting lucky!

If all else fails, liquor will certainly impress my Queen. These libations of love are guaranteed to lubricate your Mistress. If you are smart and adore her as you should, you will always have the ingredients for several of these drink recipes on hand, as they can be served alongside other recipes in this book or as a breakfast in itself.

Island Mimosa

Ingredients

- 1 ounce dry champagne
- 1 ounce Prosecco
- 1 ounce Absolut Hibiscus
- 2 ounces mango juice
- 1 ounce pomegranate juice
- Squeeze of fresh lemon juice + lemon twist for garnish

Cooking Directions

1. To a champagne flute, add champagne and Prosecco. Watch them bubble up for your Queen. Let the bubbles settle.
2. Add Absolut Hibiscus and mango juice.
3. Slowly pour in the pomegranate juice, very slowly, so that it swirls in with color. Make it pretty for your Queen.
4. Squeeze in the lemon juice and garnish with a lemon twist.
5. Bring to your Queen in bed.

This is best if it gets to sit and infuse overnight but if there is no time, a cocktail shaker works wonders. In fact, bring the cocktail shaker directly to the bedroom while your Queen slumbers and awaken her with the gentle swish of the shaker, then serve it directly into her glass. After she enjoys the drink, perhaps she will give you a shake.

Michelada

Ingredients

- 1 1/2 cups light Mexican beer (Corona is good)
- 1/4 cup freshly squeezed lime juice, rinds reserved
- 2 teaspoons Worcestershire sauce
- 2 teaspoons hot sauce
- 1 teaspoon soy sauce or Maggi sauce
- Ice
- Salt, for rimming the glasses

Cooking Directions

1. Place enough salt in a wide, shallow dish to cover the bottom.
2. Rub the rims of two glasses with the reserved lime rinds and dip them into the salt.
3. Fill the glasses with ice and set aside.
4. Place lime juice, beer, Worcestershire sauce, hot sauce, and soy sauce in a pitcher and mix well.
5. Pour into the prepared glasses, top with a few grinds of freshly ground black pepper.
6. Bring to your Queen in bed.

Instead of tomato juice for a Bloody Mary, the Michelada incorporates beer. Some days my Queen is a beer lady, which I adore. At brunch time, when she wants a Michelada served in bed to get her day started, I know I'm in for a wild ride.

Additionals...

A perfect breakfast or brunch is a tried and true ways to work your way into your Queen's heart, but it shouldn't end there. Here are some other methods to please her all the more.

Keep the Kitchen Clean

Your Mistress does not like a dirty kitchen, and she should not have to clean up after you or view your mess. After you serve her breakfast in bed, be sure to scrub-scrub-scrub and put everything back in its place.

Presentation

Your Queen is gentle and artful. Show her that you care by setting the food onto the plate in a pleasing manner. Add splashes of color with fruit or chopped herbs. Think garnish. Carry her those treats on a pretty little tray that she can prop over herself and eat while she leans back on her favorite pillow.

Also, you yourself are part of the presentation. Consider investing in a Fireman Helmet and a pair of sturdy suspenders, or perhaps a stylish hat with a leather vest. Or, completely nude is always a favorite. And, if you have back hair, PLEASE trim it, unless of course your Mistress prefers it, then leave it on so she'll have something to grab onto.

Copyright

All Rights Reserved. Copyright © 2014 Red Chili Press.

No part of this book may be reproduced or transmitted in any form or by any means, graphic, electronic, or mechanical, including photocopying, recording, taping or by any information storage or retrieval system, without the permission in writing from the publisher or from the Queen herself.

45348030R00060

Made in the USA
Lexington, KY
24 September 2015